Worcester Porcelain
in the
Colonial Williamsburg
Collection

Part of a nearly complete Worcester tea and coffee service with blue scale decoration in an exhibition building at Colonial Williamsburg.

A Wallace Gallery Decorative Arts Publication

Worcester Porcelain in the Colonial Williamsburg Collection

By
Samuel M. Clarke
Overview of English Porcelain
by John C. Austin

The Colonial Williamsburg Foundation
Williamsburg, Virginia

WILLIAMSBURG DECORATIVE ARTS SERIES, Graham Hood, *Editor*

COVER: Chestnut basket and stand, 1765 – 1775

Photography by Hans E. Lorenz; Book design by Richard J. Stinely

This book was printed in Hong Kong

Foreword

THE opening of the DeWitt Wallace Decorative Arts Gallery in 1985 presented Colonial Williamsburg with extraordinary opportunities to exhibit elements of its remarkable collections and make available the results of its continuing research. We take pride in presenting our work (and our holdings) in ways that are suited to the lay person as well as the scholar, to child and adult, in a variety of media. This book on Worcester porcelain is the second in a new series of well-illustrated works that will serve our daily visitors and our large community of friends and supporters as an introduction to the subject and a record of what may have especially pleased them in the Gallery.

Porcelain was the fashion, fad, and rage of the eighteenth century, and factories sprang up everywhere to try and satisfy the apparently insatiable demand. Worcester was particularly long-lived in the history of English factories and highly productive compared to many more ephemeral efforts. Worcester porcelain was undoubtedly in Williamsburg in the colonial period (fragments have been found by our archaeologists) but probably not in the quantity or the delightful diversity seen in this book. Winsome forms, enchanting profiles, exquisite colors, and lovely decorative designs abound in this genre, gladdening the eye and uplifting the spirits.

To Samuel M. and Polly N. Clarke and Louise W. Coon we are deeply indebted for their great kindnesses. Many of their pieces are included in this book. Sam Clarke developed an enthusiasm for Worcester in mid-life and studied it as fervently as he collected it discerningly. Much of the information herein is his contribution, too. John C. Austin, long Colonial Williamsburg's curator of ceramics and glass, has contributed much of his extensive knowledge and unquenchable passion for this fragile and lovely material in this and other books, both published and in preparation.

GRAHAM HOOD
Chief Curator

English porcelain in the DeWitt Wallace Decorative Arts Gallery.

English Porcelain
by John C. Austin

PORCELAIN, a refined, high-fired ceramic material, was first produced in China more than a thousand years ago. The material that developed in the Orient over the years was mainly what today is called hard-paste porcelain, which is made of two forms of decomposed granite, kaolin and petuntse. The secret of oriental porcelain did not reach the West until early in the eighteenth century when it was developed in Meissen, Germany, by Johann Friederich Boettger under the patronage of Augustus the Strong. The formula soon spread throughout Germany and Austria and continues to be used there today.

An "artificial" or soft-paste porcelain had been developed in France during the last quarter of the seventeenth century at Rouen and St. Cloud. It was composed of a glassy frit mixed with a potter's clay. This formula became popular at the French factories that sprang up during the eighteenth century, among them the important factory of Vincennes-Sèvres. Hard-paste began to be used at Sèvres during the last three decades of the 1700s, but it did not completely replace soft-paste porcelain until the end of the century.

French glassy frit porcelain found its way to England and became the formula used at the first successful English porcelain factory founded at Chelsea near London about 1745. Glassy frit and two other types of soft-paste porcelain were used in England during the second half of the eighteenth century. In addition to Chelsea, Longton Hall used the glassy frit variety during all ten years of its existence. Factories established at Bow (near London) and Derby also initially produced the glassy frit variety. They eventually switched to a porcelain with a bone-ash base.

The bone-ash variety of soft-paste porcelain was first used at Bow and was soon adopted by the other factories, becoming the major type in use in England at the end of the century.

Soapstone porcelain, the third variety of soft-paste porcelain, was first used at a factory at Bristol about 1750 and shortly thereafter at Worcester, which took over the earlier smaller factory. Several factories in the city of Liverpool and the Caughley factory in Shropshire started using the soapstone paste although they eventually changed to bone ash. A limited amount of hard-paste porcelain was produced at Plymouth, Bristol, and New Hall.

Bone-ash porcelain should not be confused with bone china, the principal porcelain manufactured in England in the nineteenth century as it is today. Bone china is a combination of bone-ash soft-paste porcelain and hard-paste porcelain in which kaolin and petuntse are combined with the bone ash made of calcified cows' hooves.

Although much English porcelain is fresh and original in form and decoration, most of it, especially during the third quarter of the eighteenth century, was influenced greatly by porcelain from the European continent, particularly from the factories at Meissen and Sèvres. Oriental influences were derived from both China and Japan although much came to England via the Continent rather than directly from the Orient. Floral decoration, both European and oriental in feeling, was used, as were other forms of nature that appeared as painted decoration and also in three-dimensional objects. Landscape and figure decoration existed in both Eastern and Western styles, while scenes from Aesop's fables were copied from books popular during the period.

Forms consisted primarily of wares for the dining, dessert, or tea table, although examples for the dressing table and washstand also existed. Most of the factories produced a few figures, but the majority came from the four "glassy frit factories," Chelsea, Derby, Bow, and Longton Hall. Many of these figures are direct copies of those created at Meissen.

The thin delicacy of porcelain was perfect for the rococo style. This fashion was interpreted boldly throughout the entire second half of the eighteenth century. Although the neoclassic style can be found in some English porcelain of the period, it never really took hold. That style was popularized through the earthenware and stoneware of Josiah Wedgwood.

In spite of influences from the Orient and the Continent and the continuous borrowing of ideas by one English porcelain factory from another, each establishment produced its own special delicate wares.

Portrait of Dr. John Wall. *Courtesy, Trustees of the Dyson Perrins Museum Trust.*

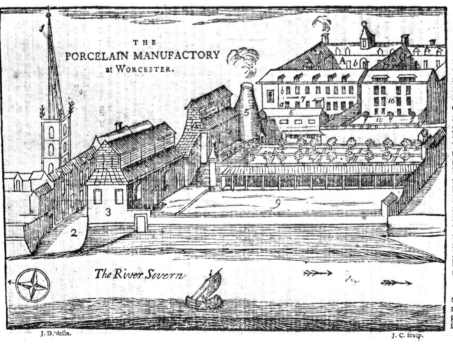

THE
PORCELAIN MANUFACTORY
at WORCESTER.

The River Severn

J. D. delin.

J. C. sculp.

EXPLANATION.

1 St Andrews. 2 Warmsley slip. 3 Biscuit kilns. 4 Glasing kilns. 5 Great kiln for segurs. 6 Pressing and modelling gallery.—— 7 Rooms for throwing, turning, and stove drying the ware on the first floor *a*, of the chamber floors. 8 The garden. 9 The yard for coals. 10 Mr Evett's house and garden, landlord of the premises. *b* The eight windows in two large chambers, in which the ware is placed on stallions, on the East and North, where are the painters rooms.——All the beginning of the process is carried on under the quadrangular building ground floor, mark'd A ; in its N. W. angle is the great rowl and ring; in the N. E. the horses turn the same, and the levigators near to the rowl. The next (on the ground floor) is the slip and treading rooms, behind Number 4 is the glasing room, behind 5 is the secret room on the ground floor.

N. B. A sale of this manufacture will begin at the *Worcester* music meeting, on *Sept.* 20, with great variety of ware, and, 'tis said, at a moderate price.

This illustration of the Worcester Porcelain Manufactory appeared in a 1752 issue of the *Gentleman's Magazine.* CWF.

Worcester Porcelain of
the Dr. Wall Period
by Samuel M. Clarke

The Company

The Worcester Porcelain Manufactory had its beginning on June 4, 1751, with the signing of a partnership deed by fifteen individuals, all but one of whom were residents of the County of Worcester. The stated purpose of the partnership was to finance the expansion of an existing porcelain works owned by Dr. John Wall and William Davis. In 1752 the Worcester company acquired the process and assets of a porcelain factory in Bristol owned by Benjamin Lund and William Miller, along with the right to mine soapstone (steatite) in Cornwall. The business was established on the site of Warmstry House, a former manor house on the bank of the River Severn near the cathedral, where the company remained until it united with the Chamberlain company in 1833. The Worcester company is the only one in England to have produced porcelain continuously since the middle of the eighteenth century.

The number and identities of the owners of the company changed several times during the first thirty years, but Dr. Wall remained a partner until his death in 1776, and Davis continued as managing partner until the company was sold in 1783 to Thomas Flight, who had been its London agent. The years from 1751 to 1783 have become known as the Dr. Wall period.

The Wares

The porcelain produced at Worcester during the Dr. Wall period was distinguished by the use of soapstone as an ingredient of the paste. This resulted in a porcelain that, while technically "soft paste," was harder and finer grained than the glassy porcelain made at

Chelsea and other English factories. From a practical standpoint its outstanding characteristic was the ability to withstand boiling water without cracking or crazing. Its use was abandoned only after the sale of the company to Flight and the substitution of a bone-ash formula essentially the same as that used today in the manufacture of "bone china."

The output of the company during the Dr. Wall period consisted almost exclusively of useful wares for the table, with only a few ornamental pieces such as vases and candlesticks, and a very small group of figures, of which only a half-dozen models are known.

The period is logically divided into four chronological Parts, in each of which the wares produced had certain distinguishing characteristics of shape and decoration:

Part I, before 1755
Part II, from 1755 to 1765
Part III, from 1765 to 1775
   a. decorated at the factory
   b. decorated at the London workshop of James Giles
Part IV, after 1775

The word *about* should be understood to precede these, and all of the following, dates. There is no documentary evidence to support this dating of the Parts, and in any event style changes would have been introduced gradually so that the Parts necessarily overlapped.

Shapes

During the earliest years (Part I), most of the production was of smaller pieces such as coffee cups, teacups and saucers, teapots, sauceboats, cream boats and jugs, small vases and bottles, and pickle dishes, although a few large pieces such as plates and vases were made. The boats are of silver shapes, with surface molding in the style of silver embossing. Teapots are globular in general outline and octagonal in horizontal section. Teacups and saucers are either octagonal or have twelve deep flutes.

In Part II the wares took on the neatly potted, well-proportioned shapes for which Dr. Wall porcelain is best known. Teapots are globular or pear-shaped, the latter of small size with faceted spouts. Coffeepots of elongated pear shape appeared and continued throughout the period. They have plain spouts, handles with a thumb rest and a kick at the lower end, domed covers, and flower finials. Plates and large jugs, mugs, and vases were also introduced during this decade. The vast majority of plates introduced then and later have either fluted borders and scalloped edges, or flat borders and twelve-lobed edges. Mugs are cylindrical and bell-shaped. Jugs are either globular, with straight necks and cabbage leaf molding, or pear-shaped. The first half of this decade includes the probable dates of the "scratch cross family," a group, mainly of mugs and jugs, that are sometimes marked with an incised saltire cross. The mugs are usually waisted cylinders without foot rims. The typical jug is pear-shaped, with a splayed foot. The family is somewhat tentatively assigned to the Worcester factory because of its soapstone body, although the shapes are atypical.

The wares of Part III included in large part "complete tea and coffee equipages," "services for desart," and "table services." A complete tea and coffee service had forty-three pieces including a teapot, cover, and stand; a sugar bowl, cover, and plate; a tea jar and cover; a milk jug and cover; a spoon tray; a slop bowl and plate; twelve teacups and saucers; and six coffee cups. The other services were made up of varying numbers of plates and serving dishes of several shapes and sizes. Shapes are generally plain, without molded ornament. One group of tea service shapes has vertical flutes, the so-called Warmstry flutes.

Figure 1. Sauceboat from Part I.

Figure 2. Teapot from Part II.

Figure 3. Teapot from Part II.

Figure 4. Bottle from "scratch cross family," Part II.

7

Figure 5. Coffee cup and saucer showing Warmstry flutes, Part IIIa.

Figure 6. Tea jar showing Warmstry flutes, Part IIIa.

Figure 7. Tea jar showing vertical ribs, Part IV.

Figure 8. Milk jug with ribbed decoration, Part IV.

The last decade of the Dr. Wall period (Part IV) is characterized by tea service shapes with vertical ribs and ear-shaped handles. Teapots are barrel-shaped, with flat recessed covers, flower finials, and ribbed spouts.

In Parts III and IV a variety of vase shapes was produced: baluster shapes with short necks and domed covers or flared mouths, sometimes with handles; ovoid shapes with short necks and domed covers; hexagonal potiches with domed covers; and the so-called Roman bronze shape with a bulge at mid-height. Jugs and mugs were made in large numbers and in several sizes.

Decoration

Blue and White. Throughout the Dr. Wall period a substantial part of the factory's output was decorated on the biscuit body before glazing (underglaze) with cobalt blue, the only available pigment that could withstand the temperature of the glazing kiln. These wares form a minor part of the collection of Worcester porcelain at Williamsburg.

Transfer Printing. The process of printing on ceramics from engraved copperplates, using moistened paper as the transfer agent, was developed and used extensively at Worcester, much of the work being credited to Robert Hancock, a well-known engraver. It was done both underglaze in cobalt blue and overglaze in enamel colors, principally black, sepia, and iron red. Pictured, among others, were portraits of sovereigns and other notables, rural scenes, landscapes,

8

usually including architectural ruins, and oriental groups in the manner of Pillement. The process was first used during Part II and continued throughout the period.

Overglaze Decoration. The pigments available for overglaze painting were all metallic salts and were restricted in number, but a remarkable range of hue and depth was obtained.

During Part I the decoration was almost exclusively Chinese in character, copied and adapted from oriental originals. It includes flowers, birds, figures, and landscapes, all delicately rendered in subdued colors.

In the next decade, although oriental decoration continued, as indeed it did during the entire period, a large part of the overglaze decoration shows German influence, with birds in naturalistic settings and loosely arranged flower bouquets, all on a plain ground. Much of this painting is by or in the style of James Rogers, who has been identified as one of the Worcester decorators. The style is distinctive, as are the bright orange and dull blue often found in his work.

The factory decoration during Part III was marked by bouquets and garlands of closely bunched flowers in the Sèvres manner, and by brightly colored, totally imaginary birds, both on plain grounds and in reserves in grounds of underglaze blue and overglaze yellow and green. A favorite use of the blue was as a ground in which the depth of the color was varied to produce a fish scale pattern. The grounds were enhanced by delicate gilding, sometimes in great elaboration.

Figure 9. Flower container with blue and white decoration, Part IIIa.

Figure 10. Coffeepot transfer printed in black, Part IIIa.

Figure 11. Funnel with overglaze decoration, Part II.

Figure 12. Vase with loosely arranged flower bouquets, Part II.

9

Figure 13. Pair of vases with totally imaginary birds, Part IIIb.

Figure 14. Plate with painting attributed to Jefferyes Hammett O'Neale, Part IIIa.

Figure 15. Plate with decoration by James Giles, Part IIIb.

Two painters with some renown in other fields, Jefferyes Hammett O'Neale and John Donaldson, decorated Worcester porcelain during this period. The former is thought to have been responsible for a series of plates and serving dishes with scenes based on Aesop's fables.

James Giles operated a porcelain and glass decorating shop in London from 1763 or earlier until 1776. Much of his work was done on porcelain purchased from the Worcester company, either in the white or with blue ground and blank reserves, and for a few years his work may have approached in quantity the overglaze decorated production of the factory. Giles's painting is noted for birds, flowers, and fruit done in brilliant colors with a broad brush, for elaborately tooled gilding on blue, claret, and turquoise grounds, and for borders of scale patterns in various shades of pink and purple.

During Part IV French influence continued, with garlands of small flowers and leaves, and berried vines, some of the latter being known as "hop-trellis" patterns. Well-drawn long-legged birds in misty landscapes also appeared. Peculiar to this decade are half-inch borders of underglaze blue of a purplish shade known as "royal."

Marks

Blue and White Wares. After about 1760 factory identification marks were used extensively on blue and white wares. By far the most common is the crescent, either open for painted pieces, or hatched for printed decoration The letter **W** and the fretted square were used rarely. There is also a great variety of workmen's marks on painted examples.

Overglaze Decorated Wares. Factory marks on overglaze decorated pieces made prior to about 1765 are rare. One exception is a small group of teacups and saucers, made probably between 1760 and 1765, the cups with everted rims and a rounded kick at the lower end of the handle, which bear a copy of the Meissen crossed swords mark in underglaze blue.

Of the items with part underglaze blue decoration, which belong to the period after about 1765, more than 80 percent bear a factory mark in underglaze blue. In the 1765-1775 decade, when the mark was a fretted square, this predominance was even greater. After 1775 the mark became first the open crescent and then a script **W**. A minor group of oriental patterns has mock-Chinese marks.

During the same period pieces decorated entirely in overglaze colors do not carry underglaze marks, with two exceptions: tea service shapes with Warmstry flutes, which usually have the square mark; and a group of identifiable tea service shapes that have the Meissen crossed swords.

Overglaze marks are rare. They take the form of red or gilt anchors or crescents and were used in connection with specific patterns, including the "Duke of Gloucester" and "Brocade" patterns.

Figure 16. Teapot with landscape decoration, Part IV.

Figure 17. The more common underglaze blue marks used by the Worcester Porcelain Manufactory.

11

Worcester porcelain in the Governor's Palace at Colonial Williamsburg. See plate 16.

The Colonial Williamsburg Collection

The Colonial Williamsburg collection of Dr. Wall Worcester porcelain covers the entire span, from the final wares produced by Lund at Bristol through the Dr. Wall period to the first productions under Flight ownership. All styles of decoration are represented, as are the many shapes and their variations. The collection is concentrated in the wares decorated partly or entirely in polychrome enamels applied after glazing. The pieces decorated entirely in cobalt blue under the glaze, and those having transfer-printed decoration, both important parts of the factory's output, are sparsely represented.

The bulk of the polychrome items is derived from two private collections. That of Mrs. Owen L. Coon was a gift to the Foundation in 1976. The pieces from the collection of Mr. and Mrs. Samuel M. Clarke were acquired, partly by gift, between 1976 and 1987. A small collection of blue and white Worcester has also recently been given to the Foundation by Mr. and Mrs. John A. Williams.

The pieces illustrated hereafter compose perhaps a fifth of the number of items in the collection. They provide an overview of the wares produced by the Worcester Porcelain Company during the three decades between 1752 and 1783, including those decorated in the London workshop of James Giles.

PLATE 1. The high-handled sauceboat formed a pair with one that is marked on the base in raised letters with the word "Bristol." It was probably made at Bristol just before the transfer to Worcester, and painted in the new factory. At least some of the other boats may have been made from molds acquired in the purchase of the Bristol plant.

15

PLATE 2. The cream boats above are distinguished from the sauceboats chiefly by their smaller size. The shape of the second from the left is the same as one in the Dyson Perrins Museum at Worcester that has "Wigornia," a Latinized version of Worcester, in raised letters on its base.

The small jugs below differ in shape from later models. They have delicately painted oriental decoration typical of the early years of the Dr. Wall period.

PLATE 3. These handleless teacups and saucers represent the three shapes produced during Part I of the period. Their decoration was always copied from Chinese examples.

PLATE 4. Small pieces like these pickle dishes and coffee cups also typify early shapes and types of decoration. The coffee cups did not conform to the teacup shapes and did not have saucers.

PLATE 5. These two pieces and the high-handled sauceboat illustrated in plate 1 are probably the earliest in the collection. It is possible that they were made by Lund at Bristol.

PLATE 6. The pieces on this page are examples of shapes continued from Part I of the Dr. Wall period, but with decoration of quite different character.

PLATE 7. The jug is notable for the acanthus leaf molding under the spout. The shape of the little teapot is very rare in Worcester porcelain.

PLATE 8. These pieces are typical of the shapes and decoration included in the "scratch cross family." The larger mug is dated 1754 on its base.

PLATE 9. These two pieces have painting of oriental derivation done during the latter half of the decade.

PLATE 10. The flower painting on these pieces typifies the work of James Rogers and his associates. The decoration on the mug is one of the many armorial patterns made to order throughout the period.

PLATE 11. James Rogers is also known for painting imaginary birds like those on these vases.

PLATE 12. The coffee cup and saucer were painted in the style known as "penciling." The tea bowl and saucer were printed from one of the earliest plates engraved by Robert Hancock.

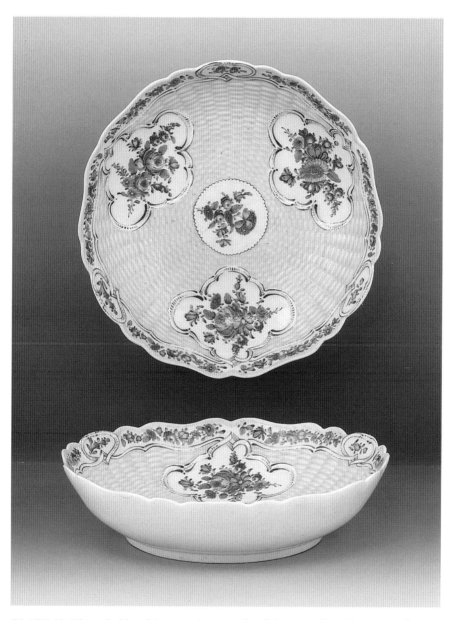

PLATE 13. The salad bowl is an early example of the use of a yellow ground.

PLATE 14. This "tea and coffee equipage," with one of the variations of the "quail" pattern, probably also included a spoon tray, a teapot stand, and a tea jar. The shapes have the Warmstry flutes.

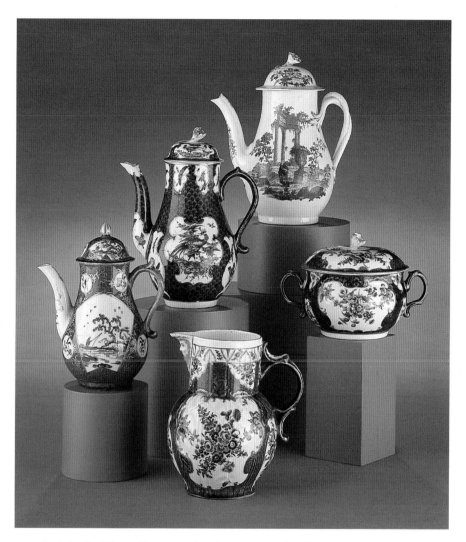

PLATE 15. The coffeepot with colored-over prints has spout and handle shapes very rare on coffeepots that are indicative of the crossed swords mark, which this possibly unique example bears. The bottom pot is decorated entirely in underglaze blue except for the gilding, and is the only pattern that has two factory marks, the square and the crescent. The pot with the "agitated" birds has exceptionally well-defined scales in the blue ground. The flower decoration on the jug and broth bowl is in the style usually found on blue scale pieces. The jug is molded in low relief with large cabbage leaves and a mask spout.

PLATE 16. The vases and the plate are delicately gilded on blue scale grounds.
The plate has one of the Jefferyes Hammett O'Neale fable paintings.

PLATE 17. The coffee cup and saucer have a ground that was obtained by applying the pigment as a powder. The ground color of the teacup and saucer is known as "gros blue." The blue paneled spoon tray has some of the factory's finest flower painting.

PLATE 18. The overglaze ground colors most used at the factory were a pea green and a yellow that varied from pale lemon to mustard. They were applied to the entire range of useful and decorative wares.

PLATE 19. The three dishes are all surface-molded with rose leaves and buds in a pattern known as the "Blind Earl." Two are decorated to conform to the molding, while the third shows complete disregard for it, a common practice with the smaller dishes.

PLATE 20. This salad bowl is molded in a pattern quite different from the smaller bowl in plate 13. The borders are of blue scale.

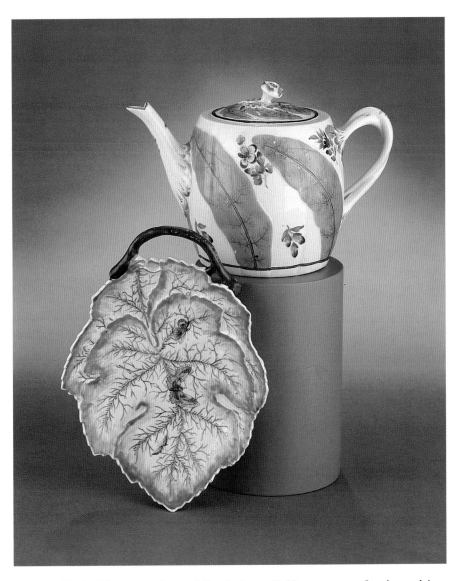

PLATE 21. The teapot has molding in low relief in a pattern of scolopendrium leaves copied from Chelsea examples. The grape leaf dish is one of the several leaf shapes made at Worcester.

PLATE 22. Serving dishes, referred to in the 1769 sale catalog as "compoteers," were made in a number of shapes and sizes. This lozenge shape and the heart shape (plate 33) were usually included in a dessert service. Chamber candlesticks were more common without piercing. The painting on this one is in a distinctive shade known as "dry blue."

PLATE 23. The pot on the right is a good example of the most common Worcester teapot shape, with painting copied from a Japanese model. The pear-shaped pot,
with twist handle and ribbed spout, is the shape that nearly always bears the crossed
swords mark when decorated all overglaze.

PLATE 24. These pieces are examples of transfer printing in black. The King of Prussia on the mug represents Frederick the Great. The pennants bear the names of his battles (mostly misspelled).

PLATE 25. Intended to be left in the single printed color, transfers were sometimes hand-decorated in various enamel pigments.

PLATE 26. The pink scale is a James Giles trademark, the same color being used in the monochrome landscape. The plates with factory-applied blue scale grounds have heavy gilding, shaped and tooled to represent foliage.

PLATE 27. These plates are examples of Giles's flower and fruit painting at its most flamboyant.

PLATE 28. The Giles-style birds on the coffeepot are similar to Meissen and Chelsea examples. Meissen influence is also evident on the small "Blind Earl" dishes.

PLATE 29. This butter tub has flower and fruit painting typical of one of Giles's workmen.

PLATE 30. The birds on the tea service of which the sugar bowl is a part are all of recognizable species. The tea jar has the "Hope-Edwards" pattern.

PLATE 31. "Sky blue" and "claret" were two of Giles's successful ground colors.

PLATE 32. These examples illustrate three of the "hop-trellis" patterns common during the decade 1775–1785. They occur only on ribbed shapes such as these. The covered porringer and stand may have been decorated in the Giles workshop.

PLATE 33. These serving dishes have shapes that were used in dessert and dinner services throughout Parts III and IV, but the patterns of decoration are peculiar to later years. The platter is from a large service thought to have belonged to William Henry, Duke of Gloucester (1743–1805).

PLATE 34. This sugar bowl and butter dish and stand show Sèvres influence. The butter dish was part of a very large service belonging in the early nineteenth century to the Earl Manvers.

PLATE 35. The teapot stand has the square mark of Part III, and the pot the crescent of Part IV, probably because the stand was made late in Part III and painted with the pot in Part IV.

49

PLATE 36. Each of the pieces on these two pages has a narrow underglaze border of a purplish shade known as "royal blue."

PLATE 37. The plate has what is called the "Lord Rodney" pattern of fanciful long-legged birds. Monogrammed mugs and jugs were a feature of the late years of the Dr. Wall period.

PLATE 38. These blue and white pieces demonstrate that such decoration was not restricted to the more mundane objects. The vases and the sauce tureen have painted oriental subjects.

PLATE 40. The majority of Worcester blue and white pieces were transfer printed from engraved plates.

54

PLATE 41. Blue transfer prints almost identical in design were used at various factories in England. Sometimes only slight variations in design or the color or paste can be used to separate factories. Sometimes only the mark can prove its attribution.

PLATE 42. These chestnut baskets with their pierced covers and stands are identical in shape and size to the one on the cover. The decoration is a combination of hand painting and transfer printing.

LIST OF FIGURES AND PLATES

57

Plate/Figure Number	Accession Number	Object	Dimension
Plate 15	G1976-171	Coffeepot	H. 9⅛″
	G1977-319	Coffeepot	H. 8½″
	G1976-196	Coffeepot	H. 8⅞″
	G1977-321	Broth bowl	D. 5⅛″
	G1976-461	Jug	H. 7″
Plate 16	1980-41	Pair of vases	H. 10½″
	G1976-470	Plate	D. 9¾″
Plate 17	G1984-290	Coffee cup and saucer	D. saucer 4⅝″
	G1977-325	Spoon tray	L. 6⅛″
	G1978-161	Tea bowl and saucer	D. saucer 4¾″
Plate 18	1980-91	Jug	H. 7½″
	1987-11	Milk jug	H. 5⅜″
	1986-7	Dessert dish	L. 10¾″
	G1984-289	Mug	H. 3½″
Plate 19	1981-32	Sweetmeat dish	D. 5⅞″
	G1976-177	Plate	D. 7⅝″
	1981-29	Sweetmeat dish	D. 5⅞″
Plate 20	L1987-645	Salad bowl	D. 10″
Plate 21	G1976-179	Teapot	H. 5¾″
	G1978-165	Leaf dish	L. 7¾″
Plate 22	G1976-467	Lozenge dish	L. 9½″
	1986-6	Candlestick	D. 5¾″
Plate 23	G1976-476	Teapot	H. 6½″
	G1976-469	Teapot	H. 5¼″
Plate 24	G1976-160	Mug	H. 3¼″
	G1976-170	Coffee cup and saucer	D. saucer 4⅝″
Plate 25	G1976-173	Teacup and saucer	D. saucer 5¼″
	G1976-486	Mug	H. 3⅜″

PART IIIb   1765 – 1775 GILES DECORATION

Plate/Figure Number	Accession Number	Object	Dimension
Plate 26	G1977-328	Plate	D. 8¾″
	1980-83	Plate	D. 9″
	G1976-211	Plate	D. 9″
	G1977-324	Plate	D. 8¾″
Plate 27	G1976-141	Plate	D. 12″
	1986-5	Plate	D. 9¾″
Plate 28	1960-313	Coffeepot	H. 8⅝″
	G1978-169	Pair of sweetmeat dishes	D. 6″
Plate 29	L1987-647	Butter tub and stand	L. stand 8″
Plate 30	G1978-179	Sugar bowl	H. 4⅝″
	1987-10	Tea jar	H. 6½″
Plate 31	1986-8	Coffee cup and saucer	D. saucer 5″
	1980-82	Teacup and saucer	D. saucer 5¼″

PART IV   1775 – 1785

Plate/Figure Number	Accession Number	Object	Dimension
Plate 32	G1977-327	Porringer and stand	H. 5″
	G1976-133	Tea jar	H. 6⅜″
	G1977-323	Teacup and saucer	D. saucer 5⅜″
Plate 33	G1976-143	Heart-shaped dish	L. 10⅛″
	1985-8	Platter	L. 11⅝″
Plate 34	L1987-668	Sugar bowl	H. 4⅞″
	1978-174	Butter dish and stand	D. stand 6¼″
Plate 35	G1979-231	Teapot and stand	H. pot 6⅜″
Plate 36	G1976-154	Teapot and stand	H. pot 5⅛″
Plate 37	G1976-200	Mug	H. 5⅞″
	1980-86	Plate	D. 8¼″

BLUE AND WHITE DECORATION

Plate/Figure Number	Accession Number	Object	Dimension
Plate 38	1953-953	Pair of vases	H. 15″
Plate 39	1973-57	Sauceboat	L. 8½″
Plate 40	G1986-231	Mug	H. 5¾″
	G1971-33	Mug	H. 5¾″
	1954-426	Mug	H. 5⅜″
	1954-425	Mug	H. 5¾″
	G1986-226	Tea service (part)	H. pot 6¼″
Plate 41	1937-170	Tureen and stand	L. stand 11⅝″
Plate 42	1954-427	Pair of baskets and stands	L. stand 9⅞″